Is Anyone Home?

A Study of the Irreplaceable Heart of the Home

By Katrece Howard

- Is Anyone Home? -

Words of Understanding Publishers

Words of Understanding Publishers, LLC

Proverbs 1:2
To know wisdom and instruction;
to perceive the words of understanding;

ISBN 978-0-9881830-4-9

Dedication

This book is dedicated to my mother, Ramona, for being the homemaker in my life. Until I had a family of my own, I took for granted the gift of the home I was blessed to have.

To my husband, William, for allowing and insisting I be the homemaker in our family. God blessed me greatly with the husband I longed for and extraordinary father to our children.

To my daughter, Lydia, who I encourage to be a homemaker in her future. There is no better work.

Prologue

I ventured writing this book knowing full well it would make enemies. Words will be hurtful to some women, memories may come back knowing they cannot be altered and there will be those to completely disagree with chapters. Putting aside the fear and rejection, I continued on because of my deep belief in helping guide the coming generations of women to the scriptures and away from culture. In no way am I comparing myself to the apostle Paul but the scripture comes to mind of Galatians 4:16 *Have I then become your enemy by telling you the truth?* I did not come from a perfect family nor claim that I am currently rearing perfect children. Having seen so much heartbreak in my lifetime of broken homes, unwed mothers and disrespectful children, the compulsion to write was overwhelming. The cure stands in front of us all but too many are blind to the obvious. Please read with an open mind.

Table of Contents

Introduction
Is Anyone Home?

Older women likewise are to be reverent in behavior, not slanderers or slaves to much wine. They are to teach what is good, and so train the young women to love their husbands and children, to be self-controlled, pure, working at home, kind, and submissive to their own husbands, that the word of God may not be reviled. Titus 2: 3-5

Homemakers are a dying breed. Like an endangered species, you see less of them each year as our culture embraces the career woman. Sadly, more care and concern attends the American Bald Eagle who was removed from the endangered species list in 2007 by the steps taken to save them. But who triumphs the cause of the "keeper at home", as stated in the King James Version, a greater majestic and needed creation? This is a subject not often taught in Bible classes or spoken of publicly since it is assumed there is no need. Young ladies today are encouraged, even expected, to attend college and have a profession whether or not they choose to marry in the future. But if they marry and begin a family, who is to rear those children? What has God commanded of parents? Can we find the authority in Scriptures to justify sending sons and daughters to other people to care for day after day instead of their mother? Do we purchase automobiles only to give them to strangers? Would one finalize a contract on a wanted house then turn ownership to an outsider? Yet many bear children then relinquish parental care asking another to tend to daily needs. How is this affecting families in the church? This study will address those Christian women who are considering secular careers or who willingly choose to be in the work force. Women who state on a resume their profession is anything but homemaker. Let us teach this coming generation of women what is meant by "keepers at home". Let us relearn the homemaker as a noble, lifelong privilege and so very paramount to family and nation. Above all, it is commanded by our Maker. This book is sincerely and lovingly written to my sisters in Christ for instruction and encouragement. It would be my prayer for them to think through decisions of motherhood and not have cause to reflect in regret.

Chapter 1 - The Myth of Feminism

The wisest of women builds her house, but folly with her own hands tears it down. Proverbs 14:1

Walking down to the bus stop on a humid morning in Florida, the girl would look back several times to see her mother confidently wave. Each school day her Walt Disney World lunch box contained a sandwich, drink and a hand written note of love with a smiling face on a napkin. When the panic of learning second grade arithmetic consistently sent her to the school nurse, her mother came to help ease the situation. Her mother was there to comfort her when the girl came home crying after saying goodbye to a fourth grade best friend moving to another state. Every day through ups and downs, sprained fingers and broken arm her mother prepared the home. I was that girl.

It will always be a cherished memory that my mother was home. She was home with me from the beginning recollections as a toddler and she was home when I came back from a day at school as I grew older. Most of the children I knew as friends in 1972 had mothers who stayed home. However, I also remember hearing of the Equal Rights Amendment. Learning that passage would mean unisex public bathrooms and women drafted for war was frightening news to a six year old. How much of that talk was misinformation can be debated, but it is part of the Feminism movement pushed on the public in the later half on the twentieth century. Women filling a role in industry left vacant by their men sent overseas in World War II brought new ideas of their status. Is being a wife and mother enough? Does a woman's life revolve around cleaning dishes and doing laundry? Could not women have a career instead of fulfilling the expected role of wife and mother?

In 1848, the revolution began rather quietly for woman's rights in Seneca Falls, New York. Ladies came together to address their dissatisfaction with certain unfair rules imposed on women. They saw themselves on the same footing with the slaves looking for freedom and the same rights which white men enjoyed without question. These women embraced the temperance issue as well, knowing the mistreatment of women was tied to drunken husbands. Two major champions of the cause, Elizabeth Cady Stanton and Susan B. Anthony, came from differing backgrounds but shared the hope of helping women's place in society. The women's plight they witnessed was imposed by men misapplying the Bible or not applying the Scriptures at all. Most men viewed woman as given for addressing their needs alone and considered them as personal property. The Bible clearly shows the role of woman at man's side: not above his head or below his foot. Both Stanton and Anthony mistakenly thought drunkenness sufficient cause to divorce in opposition to biblical teaching in Matthew nineteen. Through many years of bringing the cause to wider acceptance, the goals were achieved of fair treatment and eventually voting rights. However as the twentieth century progressed, others took up new causes, some of which did not elevate a woman's status. Instead the freedom to sin by fornication and abortion was embraced.

The myth of feminism remains in the fact that women did not gain higher ground by its achievement. Women became promiscuous. Abortion became accepted, legal and rampant. It became the final and supreme goal of feminism. The feminist movement seems to rely completely on the issue of abortion since nothing else really matters. But what was gained through its legalization? Emotional scars never healed in the decisions made by ungodly advice. The outcome of feminism varied greatly from what had been promised: equality, happiness and a better way than what God had designed. Equalization of the field between men and women changed the relationship. The liberated woman demanded to be treated as a man in all aspects of her life: financial and emotional. She also demanded to be decadent as well, to be sexually wanton and unrestrained by any moral code. Now free sexually, she can choose to sin with a clear conscience. Her life now follows the path of sexual desires. Abortion makes her biologically equal. She can walk away from any sexual relationship with no commitments to the man or a child conceived.

This sexually liberated woman also demanded respect, but sexual promiscuity destroys all semblance of esteem. Did this step bring her happiness? Feminism works at defining, establishing, and defending equal political, economic, and social rights for women. While admirable, how does sexual freedom and legalized abortion promote anything that is good? How did a movement running on economic and political issues suddenly veer into defending, promoting and demanding immoral behavior? Wickedness became a central part of feminism.

"Without something of my own, I do not feel complete as a woman. My career gives me purpose beyond my role of wife and mother. The work at my job helps me feel I am accomplishing something." Have you heard those words from women? Do you hear the pride in their voice? What is the reason for a woman feeling the need to work outside the home? Her greediness in possessing and paying for certain items? Time needed away from her children? Is she bored taking care of physical chores for the house? Does she enjoy being with others more than her family? The thread weaved in the answers is selfishness. This same thread weaves in the idea of feminism. Instead of selflessness, a feminist mind puts self before others. Her desire, wants, fulfillment and needs become the driving force of her action. This state of mind does not obey God but caters to worldliness. Paul's words of warning perfectly describe how we should regard this evil in Colossians 2:8 *See to it that no one takes you captive by philosophy and empty deceit, according to human tradition, according to the elemental spirits of the world, and not according to Christ.*

What is forgotten and ignored by the world is God's word concerning women. He has from the beginning created us to have purpose in this life. It is mankind who mistreats and misuses what God has given. We as Christians need to always keep first in our mind what God's word teaches on all matters. The world misunderstands the Bible. Collectively it believes the Bible teaches that a woman's status is relegated to a servant, slave or possession. On the contrary, women are upheld as a weaker vessel (1Peter 3:7), helper (Genesis 2:20) and heirs in the Kingdom with all the promises of life God allows (Romans 8:17). Feminism gained women nothing. Following the Bible uplifts women to great heights. The world regards certain women as great champions of the sexual revolution. Cultural anthropologist, Margret Mead (1901-1978) published studies of village life in Samoa to push the idea of sexual freedom. Based on her study of various tribes, Mead was one of the first people to suggest that male and female characteristics were a matter of culture and not only biological differences. God teaches us otherwise in His word; men and women have specific roles clearly set in scripture. Media spokeswoman for the women's liberation movement, Gloria Steinem (1934-) has championed every issue the Bible teaches against. She proudly admits to no remorse for having an abortion as a young woman. Outspoken advocate of the sexual revolution, Helen Gurley Brown (1922-2012) penned the book *Sex and the Single Girl* and was editor of *Cosmopolitan* magazine, both publications which provided guides in unrestrained behavior. These are but three remembered by awards and accolades from a willfully ignorant people. Their life's effort will help one neither enter heaven nor become a better person. However, what a woman pursues in her life by obeying the Word of God as a wife, mother and sister in Christ will ensure her of a heavenly home. As Christian women and mothers, we need to see the coming generations do not embrace the doctrine of feminism. Let us teach them to embrace and uphold the Bible.

```
UNDER
CONSTRUCTION
```

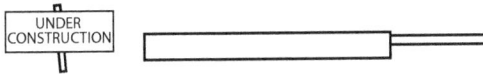

Questions to consider - Chapter 1

1. Of the women in the Bible, who would likely be a feminist? Why?

2. According to the Bible, are men and women equal in their given role? Cite the scripture.

3. Are men and women equal in the Kingdom according to Romans 8:17?

4. In Psalm 127:3, Jeremiah 1:5 and Luke 1:42, what does the Bible teach of those in the womb?

5. What does Solomon conclude brings true fulfillment to man or woman in Ecclesiastes 12:13?

Chapter 2 - Who Needs To Be Home

To Timothy, my beloved child: Grace, mercy, and peace from God the Father and Christ Jesus our Lord. I thank God whom I serve, as did my ancestors, with a clear conscience, as I remember you constantly in my prayers night and day. As I remember your tears, I long to see you, that I may be filled with joy. I am reminded of your sincere faith, a faith that dwelt first in your grandmother Lois and your mother Eunice and now, I am sure, dwells in you as well. 2 Timothy 1:2-5

In an ideal world, all married women would be homemakers. The goal of every Christian wife and mother should be to do all possible to stay home to manage the house and rear children. This sounds Neanderthal to the world. Is it the goal of this book to drag women back in time to the nineteenth century and chain them to a butter churn? Not at all! On the contrary, its purpose begs women to return to the commands in the Bible and awaken to why so much has gone wrong in our society. There is a cause and effect. Simply stated, rejecting God and His word stands the reason. The wreckage of families and flaunting of sin remains the effect. Are we numbed to its influence?

So often I hear young ladies questioned what their goals are as high school comes to an end. What do they plan to major in at college? How about law? Medicine remains a good field. Probably education will be chosen. What if she answered "Home Domesticity"? Is that offered as a major? Would that require attending college? No one considers a young lady may choose not to attend college or technical school. To do so would be wasting a mind. Why do we as a society expect that of both men and women? Sadly, too many believe "she needs something to fall back on" as though death or divorce are imminent. What does this say of our nation?

While pursuing a further education may be the right path for some, it does not need to be pushed on all. Of course, there remains the joke "She is getting her MRS degree". In attending college, I met my future husband and best friend. For that opportunity, I am ever grateful however it was not planned. My college degree has been set aside while continuing a superior degree: Motherhood.

Should a woman decide to attend college, she needs to choose a vocation she can use while remaining home in the future. An education degree can assist her in teaching her own children or offering classes to others in her home. A business degree could be beneficial in running a home based business or family company. Using her education to follow a career while on her own is reasonable, but as her life changes to wife and mother, her focus shifts to her family. If a certain field of study takes all her devotion, it would be better for her to remain unmarried (1 Corinthians 7:8). Just as the apostle Paul, her efforts can be concentrated first to the Lord then to her chosen profession.

As a young lady considers one to marry, it should be understood beforehand what she expects from her husband. She must emphasize how important it is that she remain home. She and her potential mate have to be of one mind on this. Having major points clearly discussed and mutually understood from the start will save turmoil between husband and wife and the pressure to change plans after the "I do" is said. Let us remember what God commands,

Wives, submit to your own husbands, as to the Lord. For the husband is the head of the wife even as Christ is the head of the church, his body, and is himself its Savior. Now as the church submits to Christ, so also wives should submit in everything to their husbands. Ephesians 5:22-24

So often we continue in a path by tradition, family pressure or what seems normal by the world's standard. Is that how a child of God should look at decisions? Some choices are insignificant such as buying a certain brand of cereal because of an appealing commercial. Other choices, such as deciding to work outside the home or not, are life changing and affect not only you but your family for years to come (perhaps even generations to come). Those choices need to be prayerfully considered. How crucial that you are homemakers! As we continue looking at what the Bible has to teach in the following chapters, it will be logical to see no other choice.

However, death or divorce can change the situation where it is not possible for the wife to remain home but become necessary to find outside employment. Many a new wife begins a walk with her mate only to lose him unexpectedly in death. Sin creeps into a marriage destroying the bond between husband and wife ripping apart children from fathers. In either tragic case of finding yourself on your own again, the likelihood to require a job would be high. Family may be available to help but some women would need to find a means of support or income. Those circumstances are not addressed in this chapter. Should that be the case you or a loved one confronts, I urge you to consider the chapter on home based business. This section focuses on women yet to marry, those married who plan to have children or currently have children in the home.

Perhaps a couple is unable to have children and choose not to adopt; should that woman remain home? In such a case, it is a personal decision between the husband and wife. If no children enter into that union, finding employment outside would be completely acceptable. What if the child has grown and is employed or perhaps moved away? Again, there would be no harm in working outside the home since your children are now adults. Your role as caregiver and protector is complete, though the role as caring parent remains. It is the home with very young or school age children where it is so important that the mother be present to nurture, teach, protect and guide precious souls given by God for such a short time.

For a least two generations, there has been an increase in the number of grandparents rearing grandchildren. A health issue of the parent may be the cause in some cases with disease or death. Financial problems can factor into needing temporary help from family. Although sadly in the majority of cases, the lack of good character required in the parent leads to leaving children with grandparents. High divorce rate factors into the situation with broken families scrambling to find a caregiver. Single parent homes look for another to assist with the child. Selfishly, a parent may assume their own parent can handle the rearing of the child and caters to their own desires. Mothers who continue with outside careers look to grandparents to provide trusted housing while they work. This essentially becomes free daycare.

Some grandparents agree to the arrangement thankful for the time with the child and provide excellent care. However, some take on the role as a burden. Statistics from usa.gov estimate about two million grandparents are rearing about four million grandchildren. The care of the young can become too much for one who may be twenty to forty years older than when they reared their own children. Daily needs of an infant would be harder to manage at sixty years old instead of twenty five. Physical ailments will hamper the ability to perform necessities. Retirement plans may evaporate due to the change in their life. Discipline of children wanes from physical or emotional exhaustion of the grandparent leading to unruly behavior from the child. Teenagers especially can take advantage of the situation compounded by their own feelings of neglect by mother or father. All of these elements result in homes God did not intend. Timothy was blessed in having a grandmother to help in his upbringing but his mother was also involved (2 Timothy 1:5). The role of parenting was not placed on grandparents.

Mothers need to remain home. Our Father clearly commanded the mother take care of children. It is to men the command to provide for his family was stated. In Genesis Chapter three, there is a message to the serpent, to Eve and then to Adam. *And to Adam he said, "Because you have listened to the voice of your wife and have eaten of the tree of which I commanded you, 'You shall not eat of it,' cursed is the ground because of you; in pain you shall eat of it all the days of your life; thorns and thistles it shall bring forth for you; and you shall eat the plants of the field. By the sweat of your face you shall eat bread, till you return to the ground, for out of it you were taken; for you are dust, and to dust you shall return"* (Genesis 3:17-19). The message to Adam was that of work and toil. He would be the one to provide for his family regardless of hardships. 1 Timothy 5:8 also applies to the husband (though not exclusively): *But if any provide not for his own, and specially for those of his own house, he hath denied the faith, and is worse than an infidel (KJV).* Logically this leaves the woman to be the worker at home (Titus 2:5). Leave the others to tend to business in the world. Cherish the time you are given to create a home worth more than money. Make your home rich with love, kindness and good works. Linger in the moment to smell that beautiful newborn. Stay with your child to watch every step in physical growth. Continue to be the presence needed as they grow older teaching them in word and deed. Persist in this role though there will be some who perceive your efforts as old fashioned, overly conservative even misguided. Certainly you want to assure your children have a home in Heaven! Be proactive to help it happen. You as parent navigate the waters as captain of your ship. It is your watch. Follow the commands of God being an example to all. Stay home!

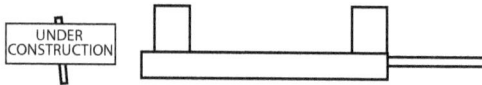

Questions to consider - Chapter 2

1. Does the Bible teach a woman cannot learn a trade? Consider Acts 18:3

2. Where should a woman's priority be once a mother?

3. According to 1 Corinthians 7:32 the unmarried cares for who?

4. What scripture teaches the man is to provide for his family?

5. Can a scripture be found commanding the mother provide for the family?

Chapter 3 - What God Commands

The wise of heart will receive commandments, but a babbling fool will come to ruin. Proverbs 10:8

Many books are written to capture the imagination of readers, to sell different products or to teach concepts to those who wish to learn. The principal book we all should read and understand remains the Bible. It contains all information of how to live this life, how to please and glorify God and how to endure until our home in Heaven. What an author declares in any subject is meaningless when spoken without the use and knowledge of God's Word. Solomon declared in Ecclesiastes 12:12 *My son, beware of anything beyond these. Of making many books there is no end, and much study is a weariness of the flesh.* This author, as well, should not be given an ounce of your time if she does not include what the Bible teaches over her opinion. Solomon concludes his thought in verse thirteen with the wise words; *The end of the matter; all has been heard. Fear God and keep his commandments, for this is the whole duty of man.* The commands of God to his creation need to be our every thought and desire. What does God command to women as homemakers? What does He expect of us as wives, mothers and servants in the Kingdom?

How do we discern if a scripture is a command or not? The Bible teaches us in 2 Timothy 3:16 *All Scripture is breathed out by God and profitable for teaching, for reproof, for correction, and for training in righteousness.* Teaching may be accomplished by direct command, example or implication. All scriptures teach us in one of these ways. In 2 Timothy 2:15 Paul tells Timothy that he must rightly handle the word of truth. What does this mean? Timothy was to know the scriptures well enough to know what applies to people under the Law of Christ and how it applies to them. Though done logically, it does take an amount of skill for the more difficult things found in the word of God. One who diligently applies the word of God in their life will learn this skill to a greater degree as they mature in Christ. This is taught in Hebrews 5:14 describing the simpler things as "milk" and the more difficult things as "solid food." *But solid food is for the mature, for those who have their powers of discernment trained by constant practice to distinguish good from evil.* We need to understand that the Law of Christ is found in the entire New Testament. It is not found only in the Gospels (Matthew, Mark, Luke and John), but the whole New Testament completes the Law of Christ. The commands of God are given by direct statement, example and implication. These are seen in action in the Bible in the lives of faithful brothers and sisters. We find a pattern of sound words discussed in 2 Timothy 1:13 *Follow the pattern of the sound words that you have heard from me, in the faith and love that are in Christ Jesus.* Also a pattern of behavior was to be followed and imitated as Paul writes in Philippians 3:17 *Brothers, join in imitating me, and keep your eyes on those who walk according to the example you have in us.* In the Great Commission in Matthew 28:19-20, Jesus tells us we are to make disciples and teach them to observe all things He commanded: *"Go therefore and make disciples of all nations, baptizing them in the name of the Father and of the Son and of the Holy Spirit, teaching them to observe all that I have commanded you. And behold, I am with you always, to the end of the age."* How can we know what applies to us today and what does not? Since we are under the same Law of Christ that the first century church was under, and since the Law of

Christ does not change, we need to do as Paul stated: "*Follow the pattern of the sound words*" and "*join in imitating me.*"

Which scriptures are direct commands to women as wives? Let us begin at the beginning. In Genesis 2:24 a direct command is made to both men and women concerning marriage, *Therefore a man shall leave his father and his mother and hold fast to his wife, and they shall become one flesh.* This verse clearly states a command to wives to understand the separate home they begin and the sexual union God created within marriage. Jesus refers to this in Matthew 19:4-6 *He answered, "Have you not read that he who created them from the beginning made them male and female, and said, 'Therefore a man shall leave his father and his mother and hold fast to his wife, and the two shall become one flesh'? So they are no longer two but one flesh. What therefore God has joined together, let not man separate."* Are these words binding on us? Correcting the Law of Moses in His answer Jesus states what is now the Law of Christ concerning marriage. This law is an eternal principle. It will never change until Christ returns and this world and the need for marriage are no more. Jesus gave a direct command concerning divorce in Matthew 5:31-32 *"It was also said, 'Whoever divorces his wife, let him give her a certificate of divorce.' But I say to you that everyone who divorces his wife, except on the ground of sexual immorality, makes her commit adultery, and whoever marries a divorced woman commits adultery."*

The apostle Paul speaks of marriage and what God commands of the wife in several epistles. Paul qualified the command was of the Lord in 1 Corinthians 7:10-11 *To the married I give this charge (not I, but the Lord): the wife should not separate from her husband (but if she does, she should remain unmarried or else be reconciled to her husband), and the husband should not divorce his wife.* Several verses within the New Testament teach a woman's place of submission in clear direct verses. Paul, by inspiration of the Holy Spirit, gives the command to the wife in comparison to Christ and the church in Ephesians 5:22-24 *Wives, submit to your own husbands, as to the Lord. For the husband is the head of the wife even as Christ is the head of the church, his body, and is himself its Savior. Now as the church submits to Christ, so also wives should submit in everything to their husbands.* This is a direct command tied to a constant condition – Christ is the head of the church and the church is subject to Him. When this is no longer the case then this law becomes meaningless. When Christ is no longer the head of the church then a husband will no longer be the head of his wife nor would he be commanded to love her to the point of laying down his life for her. When the church is not subject to Christ then the wife would no longer be subject to her husband. A simple direct statement teaches the head of the home to wives in Colossians 3:18 *Wives, submit to your husbands, as is fitting in the Lord.* A conditional phrase "as is fitting in the Lord" denotes the husband does not have the right to ask his wife to do something against the will of God. Verse nineteen and twenty continue to teach direct commands to the husband and children.

The apostle Peter teaches the same command to the wife in 1 Peter 3:1 *Likewise, wives, be subject to your own husbands, so that even if some do not obey the word, they may be won without a word by the conduct of their wives.* The subject of submission causes many women to vocalize their defiance. To be pleasing to God women must realize this is His will, just as we are to be submissive to God in other matters. James teaches this in James 4:7 *Submit yourselves therefore to God. Resist the devil, and he will flee from you.* God placed men as the head of the home. A godly wife does well to be obedient to that truth. Let us remember 1 John 5:3 *For this is the love of God, that we keep his commandments. And his commandments are not burdensome.*

What commands are given to women as mothers? In fact, when parents are spoken of, the father has the distinction of specific address to his duties. Ephesians 6:1-3 C*hildren, obey your parents in the Lord, for this is right. "Honor your father and mother" (this is the first commandment with a promise), "that it may go well with you and that you may live long in the land."* Chapter six begins with a direct command to children with implication to the parents. Children are not asked to obey when it is something outside of God's will. Great responsibility in governing well rests with the parents, both father and mother. They are to lead children in righteousness as they follow God. Then verse four specifically speaks to fathers, *Fathers, do not provoke your children to anger, but bring them up in the discipline and instruction of the Lord.* Again in Colossians 3:20 *Children, obey your parents in everything, for this pleases the Lord.* Fathers specifically are commanded in verse twenty-one, *Fathers, do not provoke your children, lest they become discouraged.* In no way does this diminish the role of the mother. By God's wisdom, mothers are taught more from examples and implication. Mary, the mother of Jesus, had a wise and tender heart. Being chosen by God, the angel tells of her favor among women. We see in Luke 2:19 *But Mary treasured up all these things, pondering them in her heart.* Mary did this after seeking Jesus in Jerusalem. She again shows wisdom in understanding her son's role on earth in Luke 2:51-52 *And he went down with them and came to Nazareth and was submissive to them. And his mother treasured up all these things in her heart. And Jesus increased in wisdom and in stature and in favor with God and man.* What can we learn from Mary? As mothers, we also should understand the limited time given with our child. With that restricted time, we need to do all possible to help them increase in wisdom and stature, giving them back in service to God. How can a woman manage this duty with outside, fulltime responsibilities as well?

Paul tells of godly women in his letter to Timothy in 2 Timothy 1:5 *I am reminded of your sincere faith, a faith that dwelt first in your grandmother Lois and your mother Eunice and now, I am sure, dwells in you as well.* The example of the grandmother and mother of Timothy is brief but sufficient to understand the type of women they were. A godly child develops by a godly mother. If Eunice was anything other than a righteous woman, Timothy may have become a good man but it would have been despite her as a mother not as a result of her being a good mother. Motherhood is an extraordinary position which the world belittles and mocks. Souls brought up protected, nurtured and taught become useful servants in God's kingdom. This does not happen by chance nor does it happen overnight. Beginning at infancy with a mother who shows deep love through her presence can raise a godly man such as Timothy. What is implied in this example? Mothers are to raise their children in the Lord.

What commands are given to women as servants in the Kingdom? First, women are to remember their role in worship. Paul instructs Timothy the command and reasoning in 1 Timothy 2:11-14 *Let a woman learn quietly with all submissiveness. I do not permit a woman to teach or to exercise authority over a man; rather, she is to remain quiet. For Adam was formed first, then Eve; and Adam was not deceived, but the woman was deceived and became a transgressor.* Paul commands the same to the church in Corinth in 1 Corinthians 14:34-35 *the women should keep silent in the churches. For they are not permitted to speak, but should be in submission, as the Law also says. If there is anything they desire to learn, let them ask their husbands at home. For it is shameful for a woman to speak in church.* Women are not to take a leadership role in worship as commanded by God. Though the world will see women as equal in teaching and serving, God prohibits their exercising authority in worship. Second, older women are to teach younger women by example and word to be of good character as taught in Titus 2:3-5 *Older women likewise are to be reverent in behavior, not slanderers or slaves to much wine. They are to teach what is good, and so train the young women to love their husbands and children, to be self-controlled, pure, working at home, kind, and submissive to their own husbands, that the word of God may not be reviled.* Make note of the older women teaching the younger to be homemakers! There is much to learn in doing this well. The list given should be enough to keep the older women occupied in teaching and the younger busy doing all they are taught for a lifetime!

Should we not as women want to be obedient in all matters? If God commands certain requirements of us, wise women would listen and comply. Our own judgment does not enter into obeying His will. The path others have chosen in heeding the wisdom of the world should not influence us in doing the same. What God commands of us as wives, mothers and servants must be our priority.

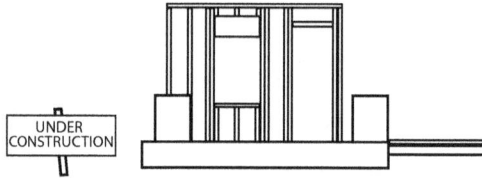

Questions to consider - Chapter 3

1. Is there a direct command to the wife? Cite the scriptures.

2. Are mothers commanded by direct statement or example? Are both ways to teach valid?

3. In 1Timothy 2:11-14, what is the reason women are to learn in silence? Does it matter what we think on the reasoning?+

4. Why are older women to teach younger women all things in the given list in Titus 2:3-5?

5. From the example of Mary (mother of Jesus) and Eunice (mother of Timothy), godly women rear their children for what reason?

Chapter 4 - Where to Look for Bible Examples

For to this you have been called, because Christ also suffered for you, leaving you an example, so that you might follow in his steps. 1 Peter 2:21

In the Bible, where can examples be found to show characteristics and qualities women can use in being a homemaker? Indeed these words would be empty if there were not examples in the Bible to learn and follow. Let us examine lives of others to garner the good and avoid the bad. Not only Bible women will be considered but also men of the Bible: Jesus' perfection, Hannah's purpose, Job's patience and Esther's providence.

Who better to begin our list than Jesus? We endeavor to be Christ-like in all walks of life; man or woman, rich or poor, doctor or homemaker. So many scriptures teach us of Jesus as part of the Godhead and how He lived as man on earth. We read this in Hebrews 2:9-10 *But we see him who for a little while was made lower than the angels, namely Jesus, crowned with glory and honor because of the suffering of death, so that by the grace of God he might taste death for everyone. For it was fitting that he, for whom and by whom all things exist, in bringing many sons to glory, should make the founder of their salvation perfect through suffering.* The Bible tells us how we can be Christ-like in love, endurance, and compassion. Again the book of Hebrews teaches us so well in Hebrews 4:14-16 *Since then we have a great high priest who has passed through the heavens, Jesus, the Son of God, let us hold fast our confession. For we do not have a high priest who is unable to sympathize with our weaknesses, but one who in every respect has been tempted as we are, yet without sin. Let us then with confidence draw near to the throne of grace, that we may receive mercy and find grace to help in time of need.* Though Jesus was not a homemaker, we can learn by His perfect life to follow in His steps.

First, Jesus was the perfect teacher. We read in Luke 6:40 *A disciple is not above his teacher, but everyone when he is fully trained will be like his teacher.* He knew when to teach, what to say directly and when to be quiet. No matter one's profession, we all need help in those areas! Teaching others the steps of salvation is required of us whether our own children or those with which we have opportunity. Jesus made use of the time He was given on the earth. Knowing the heart of mankind, He did not waste words convincing those who would not listen and obey (Matthew 7:6, John 8:3-8). One should study from Jesus to improve his or her teaching ability.

Secondly, Jesus was perfect in love for others. He loved us while we were unlovable sinners. Paul wrote in Romans 5:8 *but God shows his love for us in that while we were still sinners, Christ died for us.* Love for a nation which He knew would reject Him was shown in Matthew 23:37 *"O Jerusalem, Jerusalem, the city that kills the prophets and stones those who are sent to it! How often would I have gathered your children together as a hen gathers her brood under her wings, and you were not willing!* Jesus gave the perfect sacrifice for the saving of our souls through His death on the cross. In His love for children, He taught humility and innocence all should possess (Matthew 18:2-6). Jesus shows His compassion for those in sin as with the woman who anointed Him with fragrant oil (Luke 7:37-50).

All should strive to love as He loves us (1 John 4:19).

Third, Jesus was perfect in His example. We see this in 1 Peter 2:21-23 *For to this you have been called, because Christ also suffered for you, leaving you an example, so that you might follow in his steps. He committed no sin, neither was deceit found in his mouth. When he was reviled, he did not revile in return; when he suffered, he did not threaten, but continued entrusting himself to him who judges justly.* His example was perfect in the temptation He endured by Satan in knowing how to apply scriptures and resist evil (Matthew 4). Jesus by example demonstrated willingness to serve in John 13:15 *For I have given you an example, that you also should do just as I have done to you.* In every part of our daily walk we should show forth the character of Jesus. Hence the word Christian means Christ-like.

Hannah purposed to give back the son she longed for to God. It was in her heart before the child was born to dedicate him to be a servant in 1 Samuel 1:11 *And she vowed a vow and said, "O LORD of hosts, if you will indeed look on the affliction of your servant and remember me and not forget your servant, but will give to your servant a son, then I will give him to the LORD all the days of his life, and no razor shall touch his head."* We should purpose to do the same with our children. From the very start of our child's life, even before birth, we should do all to see that child is a faithful servant of God. Hannah placed Samuel with Eli, the high priest, to serve God at an early age. She prayed for him and continued to take care of his needs. Take note this endeavor began early! Establish in your heart your child will attend every worship service possible. Prioritize Bible matters come first before outside involvement to secular works. Show the joy in doing so.

However, godly parents do not always have the righteous children they labored in raising. While Eli's own sons did not know the Lord (1 Samuel 2:12) Samuel was ministering before the Lord as a child (1 Samuel 2:18). Samuel did not have Eli as a father having his own father and mother. His situation with Eli was to serve God by serving the High Priest. Still Hannah righteously obeyed God and with resolve guided her child's steps. Let us follow Hannah's example for our children.

Job embodies patience. Those with little or no Bible knowledge understand the phrase "he has the patience of Job". Job is referred to in James *5:11 Behold, we consider those blessed who remained steadfast. You have heard of the steadfastness of Job, and you have seen the purpose of the Lord, how the Lord is compassionate and merciful.* The King James Version uses the word patience instead of steadfastness. Patience is necessary in so many ways for homemakers. Managing a home, serving the needs of a family and caring for children can strain nerves. Too much expected of yourself or others can leave you upset and angry. Though we may never encounter the hardships of Job, we should recall the scriptures of how he handled the suffering in Job 1:22 *In all this Job did not sin or charge God with wrong.* Job did question why the events fell on him but remained true to God. Sadly, the same cannot be said of his wife who had no compassion on her husband but gave him thoughtless advice. He teaches her in Job 2:10 *But he said to her, "You speak as one of the foolish women would speak. Shall we receive good from God, and shall we not receive evil?" In all this Job did not sin with his lips.* We learn the reason for and outcome of obtaining patience in James 1:2-4 *Count it all joy, my brothers, when you meet trials of various kinds, for you know that the testing of your faith produces steadfastness. And let steadfastness have its full effect, that you may be perfect and com-*

plete, lacking in nothing. Undoubtedly, we will never encounter the trials Job endured but should learn by Job's example to handle our adversities.

God's providence runs through history. Providence is defined as divine guidance or care; it is God's power behind the scenes sustaining and guiding human events. Esther used her providential position as queen to speak to the king and save the Jews. Can it be said we as homemakers are in the position we find ourselves to do the will of God and save our children? Will we be home to fulfill that position? Mordecai's words encouraged her in Esther 4:14 *"For if you keep silent at this time, relief and deliverance will rise for the Jews from another place, but you and your father's house will perish. And who knows whether you have not come to the kingdom for such a time as this?"* Esther cast aside her fear to act on behalf of her people. Do we see the neighborhood we live in as an opportunity to do right? Can we recognize the prospect of those we come in contact with to teach them God's word? Paul reminds us of God's providence in Romans 11:33-34 *Oh, the depth of the riches and wisdom and knowledge of God! How unsearchable are his judgments and how inscrutable his ways! "For who has known the mind of the Lord, or who has been his counselor?"* As frustration develops in corruption of governments, God's providence will rest our mind as taught in Daniel 5:21 *…the Most High God rules the kingdom of mankind and sets over it whom he will.* Be courageous as Esther and stand with God using the unique position you are given.

Examples found in the Bible illustrate good and evil, perfection and flaws, love and hate, mistakes and correction. God gave us His word for a perfect reason. In Romans 15:4 *For whatever was written in former days was written for our instruction, that through endurance and through the encouragement of the Scriptures we might have hope.*

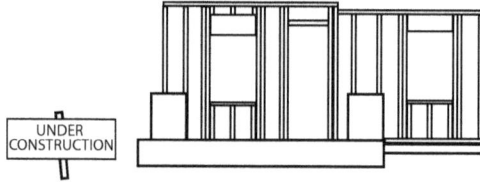

Questions to consider - Chapter 4

1. In John 13:15 Jesus' example was that of what to whom?

2. Does the Bible show examples of parents who did not rear godly children? Give other examples from the Bible.

3. With patience Job accepted his trials but did he question why? Have you impatiently questioned why trials have come in your life?

4. What is the definition of providence? Can you see providence in your life?

5. What is Paul referring to in "whatever things were written in former days" in Romans 15:4?

Chapter 5 - How to Fill Your Day with a Fulfilling Life

By wisdom a house is built, and by understanding it is established; by knowledge the rooms are filled with all precious and pleasant riches. Proverbs 24:3-4

All people possess the same twenty four hours in a day. Some run non-stop from dawn to dusk, never feeling as if they accomplished their goals. Others mindlessly walk through a job day after day, missing the joy and purpose they should have. How can a woman choosing to stay home be satisfied with a job well done as she pillows her head at night? After all, how much fun can one have scrubbing floors, loading dishwashers and doing laundry? The secret lies in the attitude behind the work.

In the Disney film, *Snow White*, the title character sang "Whistle While You Work" to the forest friends which kept her company during her temporary position of housekeeper for the seven dwarfs. It is good advice. The song on her lips was evident in her heart. Any work transforms with ease when you have the right mindset. God created woman to care for her family in the home she maintains. Let us consider how to do this day after day, year after year with joyful conviction.

Begin by a thankful prayer for another day with which you have been blessed. Never forget each day, even each minute, is a gift of God. How easy to lose sight of that simple truth! Psalm 118:24 reminds us *This is the day that the Lord has made; let us rejoice and be glad in it.* Another start presents itself to make the most of the opportunities you may find. Be cheerful and fun in the morning. Send your husband off with a kiss and in good humor to begin his day. If young ones are home, take time to show them how loved and wanted they are. Watch birds from the window during breakfast while talking about the Creation week. Sing Bible songs in the car when running errands and stave off arguments between siblings. Have a picnic in your yard breathing in the spring air and watching butterflies. Let children draw flowers and trees to be displayed in your home from a place of honor. Children need to know they are loved which can only come by spending time together. You will wake one morning to a quiet home and wonder how eighteen years vanished.

So teach us to number our days that we may get a heart of wisdom. Psalm 90:12

How do you fill your day? Find those sick and elderly who are in need of assistance. Do they need cleaning done in their home? Can you prepare meals for those bedridden? Would fresh flowers from your garden cheer someone dealing with difficulty? Involve your children to instill in them a life of service. They will learn love for others in the process. Friendship cultivated of young and old benefit both immeasurably. The aged can use the opportunity to teach wisdom and share experiences to the younger. Children will gain insight and hear memories from a time unknown to them of simpler days. Too much comes too easy for our generation. We all need to learn of sacrifices which were made by others. It is good for all. We learn service in James 1:27 *Religion that is pure and undefiled before God, the Father, is this: to visit orphans and widows in their affliction, and to keep oneself unstained from the world.*

Teach your children household duties such as cooking, cleaning and repair. They will find it fun as a child and will be of help around the home as they grow older. What future wife would not be thankful for a husband who knows how to cook? What husband would not be grateful for wife who is willing to help with yard work? These skills are best learned young before attitudes develop and while new ideas seem nothing but exciting adventures.

Take time out of the day to just be together. While showing your child their importance, you relieve stress as well. Make a pot of tea and read a classic book on rainy days. Stop the laundry and put on an old movie. Play a board game for the afternoon. Discover new favorites in classical music. Put dinner preparation aside and take a walk. It all will be there when you return. Instead of rushing through chores in haste and exasperation, your child sees their worth by you taking time for them. My father-in-law says a washing machine added twenty five years to a woman's life. Perhaps difficult to establish as fact, the idea is accurate. Woman should be thankful to have the number of modern conveniences to free them from historically laborious chores. The time taken to spend together can easily be made up in modern washers, microwaves, and vacuums.

You and your children can tackle a project for your learning or the benefit of another. Gardening reaps a harvest of fruits and vegetables to share. Learning to use a sewing machine can assist others in mending or decorating. A son who mows his father's lawn can use that skill to mow a neighbor's yard when needed. Carpenter handiness helps one in need of simple jobs around the house.

When the head of the home returns at the end of a work day, a good dinner prepared with pleasant conversation rewards him. Do not jump right into every frustration you encountered. Instead, share what good was accomplished and efforts which are ongoing. Allow him the chance to unwind and relax. Urgent matters can be discussed later. Do all possible to have his kingdom (home) and subjects (children) at peace. You as queen have this ability. His home should not be a cold stone castle but a warm inviting cottage. A godly home is not to be thought of as a shed to house material possessions, with a bed to sleep and table to eat. A godly home transforms a family into one purpose. Love and unity live inside protecting as a castle wall so the home remains impenetrable. Guard your home!

With dishes washed and kitchen clean, parents and children join together until time for bed. Read Bible passages, answer Bible questions, watch DVDs on Christian topics to use the time in teaching and growing from His word. Occasionally, play a game or take a family outing. When bedtime, pray together as children tuck into blankets ready for sleep. Be consistent in keeping the schedule so from a young age a child learns routine. Do not allow a crying child to change your evening plans. Crying diminishes as one learns a regular pattern. Parents must have sleep to function the following day, so remain firm. Father and mother transform to husband and wife needing the time alone to bond and focus on each other before another day begins. But what a day!

Can you see how much can be accomplished in one day? Individual creativity makes endless ideas in what your family achieves together. The main point is you are together. Mother stays home to make the most of each day, every opportunity and any occasion. Do not misunderstand. Days will come when the last thing on your mind may be staying together. Sometimes we all need to put space between each other to regroup and recharge. Overall, being home becomes a privilege of motherhood. She loves her children in the home she carefully creates. Service for others benefits her and her children. Good work produced fills her day. Her life is fulfilled in the love she gives to all. She has much to be thankful for and lives the words of the beautiful psalm written by David in Psalm 100:1-5.

A Psalm for giving thanks.
Make a joyful noise to the LORD, all the earth!
Serve the LORD with gladness!
Come into his presence with singing!
Know that the LORD, he is God!
It is he who made us, and we are his;
we are his people, and the sheep of his pasture.
Enter his gates with thanksgiving,
and his courts with praise!
Give thanks to him; bless his name!
For the LORD is good;
his steadfast love endures forever,
and his faithfulness to all generations.

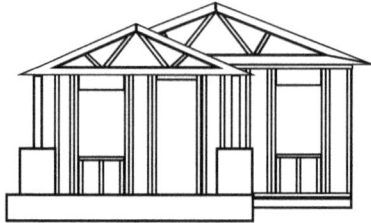

Questions to consider - Chapter 5

1. Through what is a house built and rooms filled with riches according to Proverbs 24:3?

2. What is pure religion according to James 1:27? Would a wise mother instill this in her child?

3. Why should we learn to number our days?

4. Did Jesus need time away from others during His ministry? Consider Matthew 14:13

5. At the end of chapter 5, the author mentions the main point is what?

Chapter 6 - Why Homemakers Are Needed More Than Ever

This is the exultant city that lived securely, that said in her heart, "I am, and there is no one else." What a desolation she has become, a lair for wild beasts! Everyone who passes by her hisses and shakes his fist. Zephaniah 2:15

Woe to her who is rebellious and defiled, the oppressing city! She listens to no voice; she accepts no correction. She does not trust in the LORD; she does not draw near to her God. Zephaniah 3:1-2

Is Zephaniah speaking to Americans in the twenty-first century? Although this prophesy was to the nation of Judah, the words definitely fit us today. We all study scriptures and realize how a certain passage relates to a part of our life. Every Christian should take the word of God and apply those truths. But there are scriptures in which the content seems to be taken from the daily newspaper or could be heard on a television broadcast. Hosea, Amos and Micah warn the northern and southern kingdoms of impending doom because of disobedience. Yet, the people of God committed evil regardless of the number of prophets who told them of their nearing fate. Lessons can be learned from the Bible whether in direct statement or example of others.

Psalm 78:1-8 *Give ear, O my people, to my teaching; incline your ears to the words of my mouth! I will open my mouth in a parable; I will utter dark sayings from of old, things that we have heard and known, that our fathers have told us. We will not hide them from their children, but tell to the coming generation the glorious deeds of the LORD, and his might, and the wonders that he has done. He established a testimony in Jacob and appointed a law in Israel, which he commanded our fathers to teach to their children, that the next generation might know them, the children yet unborn, and arise and tell them to their children, so that they should set their hope in God and not forget the works of God, but keep his commandments; and that they should not be like their fathers, a stubborn and rebellious generation, a generation whose heart was not steadfast, whose spirit was not faithful to God.*

Why are homemakers needed more than ever? Have you read the morning headlines? People digest revolting news with their cereal and coffee having become numb to each appalling story. What has happened to us? Unfortunately, there are too many parents who have disregarded the commands of God and not taught their children generation after generation. The writer of Psalm seventy-eight seems to speak directly to parents in the twenty-first century. How we parents need to heed these words! We are to tell our children the praises of the Lord, teach them to not forget the works of God and to keep His commandments. In turn, our children teach their children. There is much to learn.

Homemakers need to teach compassion. Compassion remains a commodity in short supply. Daily the news is filled with stories of hate and violence in any given city. Often the turmoil breeds within families. A mother remaining home instills this vital element in her child helping to develop it in their character at an early age. By her own example of taking care of her family, love and compassion will grow in her children as well.

Parents may indeed need this same compassion as they grow older and become unable to do simple tasks for themselves in years to come. According to the Centers for Disease Control and Prevention the average life expectancy in the U.S. is 78.7 years in 2010. Many will be granted years beyond that statistic and possibly deal with declining health issues. A child reared to understand compassion will emerge as an adult who turns compassion back towards their parents.

Nursing homes swell with elderly tossed aside as an unwanted clothing item which no longer fits. Some in the world cast away parents who have become inconvenient by putting them out of sight and mind. We see this same lack of respect toward parents in Jesus' time on the earth. In speaking to the scribes and Pharisees, Jesus rebuked them in Mark 7:10-13 *For Moses said, 'Honor your father and your mother'; and, 'Whoever reviles father or mother must surely die.' But you say, 'If a man tells his father or his mother, "Whatever you would have gained from me is Corban"' (that is, given to God)—then you no longer permit him to do anything for his father or mother, thus making void the word of God by your tradition that you have handed down. And many such things you do."* The Jews skirted around caring for their parents by claiming the money was devoted to God. They believed they found a way around God's laws and could not be held responsible for the needs of their aging parents. The Bible teaches in 1 Timothy 5:3-4 *Honor widows who are truly widows. But if a widow has children or grandchildren, let them first learn to show godliness to their own household and to make some return to their parents, for this is pleasing in the sight of God.* In the same chapter, verse eight applies to families in general, *But if any provide not for his own, and specially for those of his own house, he hath denied the faith, and is worse than an infidel (KJV).* Children are commanded to return the care for their parents as those parents cared for them. Compassion must be instilled during childhood to become part of one's character in life. A mother makes an excellent teacher of this essential element by word and example.

Hopefully, love was shown toward you as a child. Demonstrate that love toward your parents when they need you most. We are to honor and respect our parents as shown in Leviticus 19:32 *"You shall stand up before the gray head and honor the face of an old man, and you shall fear your God: I am the Lord."* We must not discard or ignore our parents as situations grow difficult. Solomon wrote in Proverbs 23:22 *Listen to your father who gave you life, and do not despise your mother when she is old.* His father, David, pleaded with God in Psalm 71:9 *Do not cast me off in the time of old age; forsake me not when my strength is spent.* All need compassion throughout a lifetime and more so as advancing years change one's ability to do for themselves.

Parents are to teach and make known the law of God to their sons and daughters. Who else will? The small amount of time during a Bible class cannot instill the Scriptures in a child to the depth they should know. Even the best Bible teacher does not have the ability to implant the Word in a child with the limited time given. Most importantly, it is not their job! Equally true, this role does not fall on a youth minister, preacher or elder alone. While others can help in teaching, God specifies the main educator. The command to instruct children is on parents. These scriptures plainly show the fact. Proverbs 22:6 *Train up a child in the way he should go; even when he is old he will not depart from it.*

Ephesians 6:4 *Fathers, do not provoke your children to anger, but bring them up in the discipline and instruction of the Lord.*

Homemakers need to provide a safe haven in this world of sin. So much around us screams degradation in movies, music and literature. Try watching classic television shows when morals were high on present day networks. You will repeatedly use the mute button during current commercials which show distain for godly principles. Children belittle simpleton parents knowing better what products to purchase in these thirty second advertisements. Better yet, turn off the networks and cable service. Use the television only for carefully chosen DVDs. Computers and internet allow the worst of influence instead of being used for the intended good. The unknowing click of a computer mouse can damage an innocent mind forever. Unmonitored devices dump trash into your home like the garbage trucks to the local landfill.

To keep abreast on daily news in your local community, you must sift through stories of such horror and unspeakable acts. In our home, it has become a necessity to quickly look for any information needed then throw out the paper before our children see the morning headline. Must they read about a man arrested for lewd acts in the local department store with all the details pertaining to it? No, they do not. Do we as parents have the responsibility to shelter our children? I firmly believe we do! Young children should have the luxury of remaining innocent. As they mature they will learn of the dangers in the world soon enough. Let them enjoy the years where their only thought is with which toy to play.

Undoubtedly, situations arise where a parent needs to clarify a word heard, a video clip seen, a story read. The homemaker will answer immediately. A song sung which should not be on the lips of our children, she corrects and gives understanding. Proverbs 29:17 *Discipline your son, and he will give you rest; he will give delight to your heart.* She reminds the child of scripture, principles and what God expects of His people. What could be harmful in a child's future is dealt with swift action. She handles it because she is home. Proverbs 29:15 *The rod and reproof give wisdom, but a child left to himself brings shame to his mother.* The homemaker promptly disciplines a disobedient child. Action is not delayed or forgotten because of a busy career schedule. Knowing her role as mother, this responsibility she takes seriously and desires to obey God and do the best for her children. A child left to himself brings shame with the continual trouble they encounter in behavior towards his parents, siblings or those outside. Immediate and consistent discipline teaches the child respect and love as shown in the Bible.

Proverbs 19:18 *Chasten thy son, seeing there is hope; And set not thy heart on his destruction. (ASV 1901)*

Philosopher George Santayana said "Those who cannot remember the past are condemned to repeat it." While this aphorism is often quoted, one cannot escape the accuracy of the statement. Should we not learn from others' mistakes? Do we not learn from the wickedness in the world? Are we not to learn from examples in the Bible? One cannot learn righteousness if they are not taught. One does learn from bad behavior of others whether they choose to abstain or join in.

In Amos 8:11, the prophet states to Israel the eerie message we all must remember, *"Behold, the days are coming"* declares the Lord GOD, *"when I will send a famine on the land— not a famine of bread, nor a thirst for water, but of hearing the words of the LORD.*

Stay home to teach your children the Bible. Feed them on the Word of the Lord while you have opportunity. Do not allow a famine in your home.

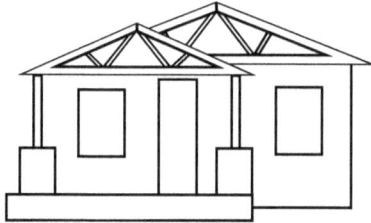

Questions to consider - Chapter 6

1. Are we different today than the children of Israel who would not listen to God's commands? Will we also suffer the consequences of our disobedience?

2. The scriptures teach the command to instruct children is given to whom?

3. Proverbs 29 teaches parents to do what to their children? If the state says a parent cannot, who are we to obey?

4. Name ways we allow a famine in our home.

5. Can we skip a generation in teaching God's word according to Psalms 78: 1-8?

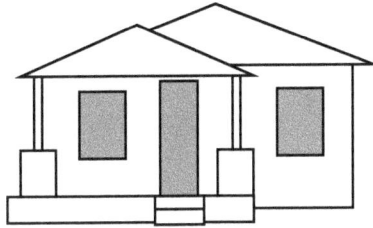

Questions to consider - Chapter 7

1. The Hebrews writer teaches us He who built all things is who? To what is the writer making a comparison?

2. Name the institutions God created.

3. Jesus teaches us in Matthew 5:16 that our good works will help others do what to whom?

4. A godly wife remembers what verse in Ephesians 5?

5. What are the three purposes of the home mentioned in chapter 7?

Chapter 8 - Strengthening the Home Will Build Up a Nation

I can do all things through Christ which strengtheneth me (KJV). Philippians 4:13

It sounds naive to believe through closer family ties and with stronger homes a nation can achieve more. What do we find out in the world in most families? Absent fathers, working mothers and children out of control with outrageous behavior. Even though the breakdown of the home becomes the debate and discussion in the world, few have the right solution. How would having more close knit families change the way a government runs? How could the family affect how a nation votes? Yet, what if all families in that nation followed the Bible by having the father God intended? Would there be a vast improvement if mothers were homemakers and disciplined children from the start? Could we see a difference in our land if children obeyed their parents and were taught to respect those in authority? The Bible clearly teaches this and we, as a nation, suffer the consequences for generations of neglect.

One can rationalize unhappy situations in a family and place blame in various directions. How easy to lay the cause on circumstances around us or influences in the world! Let us stop blaming or ignoring these conditions and take the steps to turn our nation in the right direction. Where to begin? Home. It is the word spoken and place remembered which conjures thoughts of caring, safety and love. The home is made of essential elements. First needs to be a love and respect for God's word. Seeing that word is taught to every member is necessary to a happy home. Hosea warned Israel the coming destruction for not teaching God's word to their families in Hosea 4:6 *My people are destroyed for lack of knowledge; because you have rejected knowledge, I reject you from being a priest to me. And since you have forgotten the law of your God, I also will forget your children.* You cannot expect people to live what they have not been taught. Teaching begins at home.

Who should teach? Parents are to teach their children but specifically fathers should take the lead. A father taking the God-given responsibility of teaching his family is a crucial step in having a home as our Maker commanded. As sad as it is to consider, children without fathers live a life hampered. A good earthly father helps in understanding our Heavenly Father in scriptures.

Psalm 103:13 *As a father shows compassion to his children, so the LORD shows compassion to those who fear him.*

Matthew 7:9-11 *Or which one of you, if his son asks him for bread, will give him a stone? Or if he asks for a fish, will give him a serpent? If you then, who are evil, know how to give good gifts to your children, how much more will your Father who is in heaven give good things to those who ask him!*

God meant for children to have fathers to guide their steps. He takes the lead in training.

Ephesians 6:4 *Fathers, do not provoke your children to anger, but bring them up in the discipline and instruction of the Lord.*

Proverbs 1:8 *Hear, my son, your father's instruction, and forsake not your mother's teaching,*

Proverbs 3:12 *for the LORD reproves him whom he loves, as a father the son in whom he delights.*

      Spouses remaining together for life are rare. I know of only a handful of couples to reach fifty years of marriage. Only one couple I have been privileged to meet attained seventy years of wedded bliss. Long lives were granted to these blessed mates but through love and endurance they completed the milestones. The Bible clearly states God hates divorce in Malachi 2:16 *For I hate putting away, saith Jehovah, the God of Israel, and him that covereth his garment with violence, saith Jehovah of hosts: therefore take heed to your spirit, that ye deal not treacherously (ASV 1901).* Too easily spouses cast aside the vow spoken on their wedding day. Divorce statistics vary with studies projecting almost half of those married will separate and divorce. Some feel those numbers do not accurately present the truth and the studies sound worse than they should. Still, do we not all know many families affected by divorce? It is prevalent in the world and finds its way into the Lord's church.

      We as God's creation must live what He commands of the married. To begin, one must be assured of choosing the right mate. Time and maturity enter into this monumental decision. "Marry in haste, repent in leisure" voices an idiom thought as true. It would be more accurately stated "Marry in haste, regret for life". The ties made in marriage intertwine until death affecting those around you. Choose carefully. Above all, choose a man of godly character and faith. Believe those who teach that a man will not change because of being married! I cannot say how often I taught teen and young lady's classes to see those same girls marry and divorce within a few years. Some of the girls tragically do not marry but give birth to children out of wedlock. Another path some chose would be to marry a mate who does not share faith in God. Be the example to an unbelieving husband or and win their soul to the Lord (1 Corinthians 7). Families must remain as one to fight Satan and evil influences. Congregations would grow from strong godly examples of the members to those outside in need of Christ. Do not underestimate your Christian influence. When the Lord's church behaves the same as the world in practice such as divorce, it will teach no one.

Women must consider the possibility of an affair in the workplace if they insist on having a career. Current statistics shows 46% of unfaithful wives and 62% of unfaithful husbands have had affairs with co-workers. Strong friendships develop through employment and lead to emotional ties within a daily routine of working with the opposite sex. Business travel only makes betrayal easier when away from home and opportunities abound. How dangerous to have a friendship with a co-worker which develops into a stronger bond than your spouse! Things can go wrong quickly when innocent office camaraderie breeds infidelity and the destruction of your home. Most marriages do not survive unfaithfulness with 65% ending in divorce when adultery is the cause. Why gamble with your marriage if you are able to remain home and focus on your family?

We as a nation must have mothers who see the benefits of homemaking and puts their family's well-being above their own desires. Striving to do all possible to rear children as the Word instructs makes the communities needed in our land. An expanding number of mothers at home would raise stable, happier children. The work force would not suffer from a lack of women, specifically mothers, but adjust. Conversely, the home and nation would benefit greatly from such a shift in priority. Obeying God's commands blesses homes with parents and children united in service to Him. Children trained properly would be better citizens working for the good of their family and country. Before we began our family, my spouse told me it was time to leave one job for a greater work where there is no true substitute and no one better qualified – the calling to become a mother to our children. The two of us were simply repeating the same decisions made by our respective parents. With thankful and grateful hearts we obeyed our husbands. Nations will strengthen when more women do the same.

Consider the stability in our neighborhood, communities and expanding to our nation if families remain united. Neighbors cultivate friendships as years pass leaning on each other for help. Businesses would stay together and flourish not torn apart by strife and turmoil. Candidates of good character would be the choice for office in our land. Political campaigns would have no need to rake up past events in one's background for there would be none. Laws established with Biblical guides would help all people. No abortion, homosexual rights or same sex marriages for all would use the Bible as the rule and law. Let us never forget Proverbs 14:34 *Righteousness exalts a nation, but sin is a reproach to any people.*

A beautifully written hymn by Baylus Benjamin McKinney, *God Give Us Christian Homes*, speaks of the homes God instructs us to have. Each part mentioned of Bible, father, mother and children construct the godly home taught in His word. Every home should have this hymn close to their heart. God has given us what we need; we need to obey and have the home He commands.

God, give us Christian homes!
Homes where the Bible is loved and taught,
Homes where the Master's will is sought,
Homes crowned with beauty Your love has wrought;
God, give us Christian homes;
God, give us Christian homes!

God, give us Christian homes!
Homes where the father is true and strong,
Homes that are free from the blight of wrong,
Homes that are joyous with love and song;
God, give us Christian homes,
God, give us Christian homes!

God, give us Christian homes!
Homes where the mother, in caring quest,
Strives to show others Your way is best,
Homes where the Lord is an honored guest;
God, give us Christian homes,
God, give us Christian homes!

God, give us Christian homes!
Homes where the children are led to know
Christ in His beauty who loves them so,
Homes where the altar fires burn and glow;
God, give us Christian homes,
God, give us Christian homes!

Questions to consider - Chapter 8

1. Hosea 4:6 teaches us who will be destroyed and why?

2. A loving father does what to his children according to Proverbs 3:12? This also applies to whom?

3. What covers one's garment with violence? Does the Bible number other things which God hates? Consider Proverbs 6: 16-19.

4. Proverbs 14: 34 teaches what exalts a nation? What is a reproach?

5. Homes as God commands will lead to what?

Chapter 9 - Considering Home Education

But as for you, continue in what you have learned and have firmly believed, knowing from whom you learned it and how from childhood you have been acquainted with the sacred writings, which are able to make you wise for salvation through faith in Christ Jesus. 2 Timothy 3:14-15

Have school at home? Teach your own child basic subjects? Why would a parent take on the task of schooling their children if they are not a certified teacher? Actually, home educating has grown in practice and acceptance in past years with each state's law easily managed. There are numerous books, websites, seminars and support groups to help understand how to school at home. I joyfully home educate my children but do not push those convictions on others. Yet much misunderstanding still exists regarding the difficulty of teaching and skill needed for a parent to adequately guide their children.

Imagine beginning your day waking with the sun and gathering around the breakfast table to discuss what adventures lay ahead. No child gulping frozen waffles and racing to catch the school bus to spend most of the day elsewhere. There is time to talk about studies which your child excels at and subjects they may struggle with. No rush to dress in the latest styles to impress classmates. In fact, chosen attire may be their favorite pajamas while reading *Swiss Family Robinson*. You map out the morning and afternoon with fun activities and simple errands you accomplish together. Grocery shopping teaches math basics, comparing skills and managing a budget. Meals are planned and produced as a family while learning tasks such as chopping, setting the table or washing dishes. Helping elderly members or neighbors with yard work or house cleaning can be done sooner during the week instead of waiting for a weekend opportunity. Compassion and self-sacrifice are traits learned by these occasions. This is the life of a home schooled family.

How is this done? You can make it as imaginative as you want. Simple tasks become a game. Any new word a child is learning becomes a song. The front of a refrigerator changes into a spelling board or art gallery. A beloved book always can be read one more time and travel again to far away destinations. Learning is all the time since time is precious and evaporates as steam from a kettle. Gather those opportunities while you can and make the most of each second. Any traveling in the car should be harnessed to review the alphabet, math facts or Bible lessons. The age of your children does not matter for we all should continue learning whether four, thirty-four or sixty-four. A homemaker who is filling her day to the maximum is truly exhausted by bedtime but eager to start again with new journeys for her family. What do you want your children to recall as adults? McDonald's as their favorite fast food or meatloaf a mother and daughter made together? Racing to school functions or reviewing Bible lessons at the kitchen table? Routinely watching mindless television after dinner or talking on the front porch? We all remember different times in our childhood as wonderful or unhappy. Make sure every day is a day you live as if your last. Strive to give your children the best of all; love of family, love of learning and love of the Bible.

Deuteronomy 6:7 *You shall teach them diligently to your children, and shall talk of them when you sit in your house, and when you walk by the way, and when you lie down, and when you rise.*

This process comes easier to those home educated. A mother who home schools has one on one communication with her student even should she be blessed with five children. There is the time to cultivate the love of learning. With the ability to teach Bible as a school subject, it is on the forefront and not put to the side or forgotten as other lessons take precedent. You, as parents, have the final say of what is taught to your children, the student. Can parents affirm that privilege with a school board?

You taught your child to eat with utensils, walk, talk and, more important, listen. From you they learn basic bathroom skills. Why can you not teach them to read, count numbers and memorize books of the Bible? Then move on to learning states and capitals, parts of the human body and adding and subtracting. By small steps we all learn more. Let us look at facts through logic and faith. The first fact is: reading is fundamental in education. God has communicated to man through His word preserved through the ages in written form. He expects us to read and comprehend it. The second fact follows: learning to read is entirely natural. With the ability ingrained in us, we are created with the talent to read. This talent must be developed with some children advancing faster than others. The next fact concerns the work and design of the home. God created the home and it must then function by faith in Him. It was established with its complex inner workings of father and mother and the parts they play in the lives and development of their children. These two souls are abundantly equipped to begin a home. God has placed the responsibility to teach and train children on the parents alone. Thus parents are the perfect teachers for their children. They understand their child better than anyone in personality, strengths, weaknesses, loves, quirks, and all else. No other person, however well trained, makes a suitable substitute for the parent. Since God gave the responsibility to parents and He set the pattern of the family, to suggest parents could never be qualified to teach their own children would be wrong. It would be a complete lack of faith in God's ability to structure the family.

Mothers do not become so by possessing a master's degree. She learns by doing the acts necessary of caring for a newborn. The same holds true with home education. You begin with basic understanding and learn as you go along. Children develop differently due to the sibling make up in the family. Our daughter used her Fisher Price van to transport the toy family members along with Darth Vader in the passenger seat and Spiderman riding in the back. I see the difference in her character by having two brothers instead of sisters as I did. Legos construct into elaborate dungeons instead of an ice cream shop as I might have done at her age. Her brothers, in turn, learn to be gentler with their sister than each other. Use these differences to their advantage in shaping character and choosing subjects to study.

What are the steps to begin home schooling? First, find out the facts in the state you reside. Each state will demand different requirements from parents and student. One state allows a parent to educate holding a high school diploma while another makes no mandate. One state requests your family be under an umbrella school while another state does not. There are various guidelines in regard to attendance and testing. You must know these details and comply. Contact your county school district to begin the quest. Rest assured; the facts are easily found. An organization many parents find comfort in is the Home School Legal Defense Association. Since 1983, this group works tirelessly to maintain and improve the right to home educate children. Its website can answer questions on specific rules and legal matters: www.hslda.org.

Second, find if any in your home congregation or area congregations presently home school or home schooled in previous years. There will be a wealth of information to glean speaking with a home schooling mother. Advice may be offered in methods, curriculum, expense, scheduling and many other areas. Although helpful, not all advice given may fit your family's needs. The process of home educating varies with individual families just as each student's learning needs vary from child to child. Relax and understand there is no perfect way to home school. Meeting these new contacts and friends has many benefits. Many mothers are willing to share curriculum a child has finished and exchange material. They will know the best places to find books, supplies and nearby field trip opportunities. Attending a home education seminar shows a vast array of companies and curriculum to choose from for future reference. You can see up close the many choices in the home educating market. Holding the material in your hand to determine for yourself its worth helps many new home schooling parents.

Third, both father and mother must be united in the effort to home educate. Mother at home becomes the main teacher of subjects but the father needs to be the principal. He rules as principal of the school and oversees the education process just as he rules as head of the home. Parents split in decisions regarding home education harm the teaching of children. The wife (teacher) in subjection to her husband (principal) cannot adequately conduct school if he disagrees in any aspect of instructing the student (child). It would be better if both agreed in curriculum, schedule, and method of education for their child. Fathers make excellent teachers of certain subjects perhaps the mother feels less inclined to teach. Both can become exceptional instructors to the benefit of their student and family. Agreement in home schooling creates a productive schedule, a well-adjusted child and a happy home.

Not all embark on the voyage of home schooling. In no way does it determine one's worth as a parent. Still, before dismissing the idea of home education, research the information and consider the possibility. The privilege of determining what subjects are learned and the right to choose topics make the decision easy for some. Worldly philosophies pushed by public or private schools enter into a parent's choice. False ideas taught to impressionable minds swings the pendulum in favor of schooling at home. Lies taught to a child hamper spiritual growth. It was difficult to settle in my mind as a public school student how evolution and the Bible weaved together. They do not but students to this day are forced to learn the absurd evolution theory as fact. Unfortunately, there was not enough teaching on this subject in the church during the mid-twentieth century to the damnation of many souls. You have the power as teacher to mold the mind of your student to the truth! Why not take the responsibility?

Imagine the closeness in love, the memories made, the goals achieved together by parent and child. The student will learn from the best teacher uniquely for them who loves unconditionally. This teacher has the most to gain and all to lose regarding the student's outcome. They will do everything within their power to succeed in the task taken on. This student belongs to them.

Questions to consider - Chapter 9

1. In 2 Timothy 3: 14-15 learning scripture begins during what period in life?

2. In the same passage, learning scripture makes one wise for what?

3. Must all families homeschool?

4. Do all parents need to teach their children the Bible? Cite scriptures.

5. Deuteronomy 6:7 shows teaching children should be when?

Chapter 10 - The Woman of Proverbs 31

Who can find a virtuous woman? for her price is far above rubies (KJV). Proverbs 31:10

Every Christian lady strives to be the virtuous woman spoken of in the book of Proverbs 31. She seems to be as close to perfection as a mortal can become. In the many aspects of her life from wife, mother to keeper of the home, she reaches farther than any expectation. How does she fulfill all her duties? Why does her achievement seem so unattainable to women today with all the modern convenience they possess? I submit the reason stems from women taking on roles they were not meant to have. Although the Proverbs woman has many responsibilities, these were given by God and not of her own device.

First, she is considered as wife. The trust of her husband goes beyond monetary gain into having his heart. Without trust a marriage collapses. His gain is her love for him, the care of her family and their respect in the community. One of the most beautiful verses in the Bible is Proverbs 31:12 *She does him good, and not harm, all the days of her life*. Fidelity and love is taught in one sentence. Earlier in the book, Solomon gives us a contrast between wives in Proverbs 12:4 *An excellent wife is the crown of her husband, but she who brings shame is like rottenness in his bones.* A virtuous wife brings him happiness and contentment. She is his lifelong companion and puts him first before herself. Blessings follow the virtuous woman as we learn in Proverbs 18:22 *He who finds a wife finds a good thing and obtains favor from the* LORD. In turn, he is known in the gates and esteemed by the elders of the land. He praises her and calls her blessed as we see later in the chapter.

Second, she works at home and manages a house. Look at the actions used in describing her life! She seeks, brings, rises, provides, girds, strengthens, stretches, extends, makes, supplies, opens and watches. Willing to work with her hands, she labors after sundown needing the lamplight. Using a variety of material from coarse to fine, she makes clothing for herself and her household. Her strong arms provide for her family and servants. Profits garnered by her skills return to managing her household. Purchasing fields, planting vineyards and selling her goods to merchants pronounce an extraordinary business woman. The poor and needy are not dismissed while she is able to help. Not one verse speaks of her looking for others to do her work. In fact verse twenty-seven states she *does not eat the bread of idleness*. She oversees every detail making good use of her bountiful blessings. She figuratively clothes herself in strength, honor, wisdom and kindness. No complaining of her lot, no whining to others; she does the work given to her by God. No Wonder Woman but God's woman.

Third, she is a mother. Her children proclaim she is to be respected. She reared her children well and they now express their love for her to all. They are thankful for her commitment. Tirelessly her hands work for her family and community. As mother she provides food for her family with no one hungry. Her children are clothed in scarlet and have need of nothing. By example she taught them wisdom and kindness. They learned to work and will take care of the families they will be blessed with.

Some will take a skewed view on this beloved chapter. Those who look to validate a career above staying home claim she was a business woman outside of her domain. They will site the Proverbs 31 woman purchasing, supplying, selling and profiting as business matters. It is to their justification and not by proof. She maintains a business though all work mentioned would have been produced in her home. The goods could have been sold in her home. Delivering merchandise may have necessitated her leaving the home. However, with extended family possibly living in the same house, she would have left her children in the home under watchful eyes or taken them with her. Never in the chapter is it mentioned she left her children in the care of strangers. Being a wife and mother was the ultimate goal of godly women. Sadly, godliness is not welcome in many homes today. We live several generations having been taught women must work outside the home to find self-worth, develop true potential and sustain the income. Relearning the worth of women and living the life God wants will produce more women as the one in Proverbs 31.

The chapter ends with the eloquent and truthful words in verse thirty, *Charm is deceitful, and beauty is vain, but a woman who fears the LORD is to be praised.* Many women try to slow the aging process in their vanity. Dying hair and making over imperfections only temporarily hide the truth. True beauty comes from within a godly heart. The most beautiful women in the world are not from Hollywood; they are the sisters in local congregations during their golden years. Paul instructs Timothy what becomes women in I Timothy 2:9-10 *likewise also that women should adorn themselves in respectable apparel, with modesty and self-control, not with braided hair and gold or pearls or costly attire, but with what is proper for women who profess godliness—with good works.* Graying hair and wrinkles proclaim wisdom for the righteous. The bend in her walk shows the service she delivered all her days. Her life proclaims her good works without a word. One who fears the Lord obeys the Lord. She did what God commanded and did not add to her life what the world expects. Rubies shine as beautiful gems created by God but cannot compare to a virtuous woman in His service.

Questions to consider - Chapter 10

1. Why is the phrase "All the days of her life" significant in Proverbs 31?

2. Is Proverbs 31:10 telling us a virtuous woman cannot be found?

3. Name the three roles of the woman of Proverbs 31.

4. What professes godliness according to 1 Timothy 2:9?

5. In Proverbs 12:4 "who causes shame" refers to whom? What is the comparison?

Chapter 11 - Having a Home Based Business

You shall eat the fruit of the labor of your hands; you shall be blessed, and it shall be well with you. Psalm 128:2

Stretching the dollar each month to pay necessities can be a struggle. The father works outside the home in his career providing the main source of income for the family. To help the budget expand, a second income may be needed. How can a family have the extra money without an outside job for the mother? The family's ability to have a means of income while staying home would be the ultimate solution. What kind of business a family may decide upon needs to be considered with a biblical mindset. There are many good choices for a home-based business. Choosing the one right for your situation makes all the difference.

Many positive ideas are on the side of having a home business. With research and inquiring of those with firsthand knowledge, you will see the good to come of this enterprise. First, the family sets the hours of operation for your trade and not outside management. You are your own boss! Secondly, if the store is mobile, the opportunities to travel with your family are endless. Home educated families excel in this having a more flexible schedule. Imagine the field trips and teaching prospects to embark upon! Visiting sites during off season saves your family in cost and unwanted crowds. Third, you and your children learn computer skills should the store be online. Web design skills can be taught as well to manage your own website. Fourth, to maintain a thriving business you will teach children skills in math, budgeting, accounting and merchandising. People skills develop in dealing with customers. Connections are made for future use by learning to network. Another positive point favoring home business concerns family growth. Father and son relationship nurtures in spending time together physically packing and handling merchandise. For the mother, a creative outlet is fostered to vary from housework, thus producing a better wife and mother. Sixth, extra money generated can be used for mission campaigns or other works of the church. Lastly, this venture encourages self-discipline in all family members. As mentioned in chapter two, wives and mothers who may be on their own due to circumstances can benefit greatly from running a home based business. Income is made while the ability to stay home and care for children puts her mind at ease. The burden lifts from her shoulders as she can continue to be the mother at home she desires while also providing for her family.

However, there are negative issues to consider in pursuing a home based business. Travel breaks up the routine of school, especially as a student enters higher grades should your child attend a public or private institution. Realize your child will not be home indefinitely. Eventually the workload will be left to the parent alone as children graduate and leave home. Perhaps as young ones venture out on their own, the need in extra finances would subside. A home business may have then served its purpose. Consider if you possess the character to be very organized with attention to detail and the ability to keep records. Mothers tend to have that down to a science! Overall, on a set of scales, the positive considerations outweigh the negative.

Before taking a leap in a home based business, consider these points:

1.Will my family continue to come first?

2. Do I have the time in my day to devote to a business?

3. Do I have the space in my home to warehouse needed items for a business?

4. What are the legal issues I need to understand for a business?

5. Will this venture be good for us as a family?

What business would be right for you? Do you love books? Consider owning a bookstore. Are you accomplished at sewing or crafting? A business selling your homemade creations would be perfect. Are you gifted in a certain musical instrument? You may be an excellent teacher of that instrument. Do you excel in cooking or baking some food which could be in demand? That item could be the beginning of a company. A family farm can be an outlet to sell fruits and vegetables. The knack you possess in repair work to some appliance generates into money by which many are willing to pay for the service. The ideas can be endless. Your expertise in any given area could translate into a small business which could be managed out of your home. Note the emphasis on the words "out of your home" and not to be elsewhere when children need you. That is the wonderful part of the whole idea. Though many other businesses could be mentioned, they would necessitate leaving your home to fulfill work. This book encourages you, the wife and mother, to stay home where you are needed.

Consider if the need of an increased income stems from outside pressure of the world. Remember wealth can be measured in many ways but we must use God's standard. The book of Proverbs addresses riches in the following two passages:

Proverbs 13:7 *There is that maketh himself rich, yet hath nothing: there is that maketh himself poor, yet hath great riches (KJV).*

Proverbs 30:8-9 *Remove far from me falsehood and lying; give me neither poverty nor riches; feed me with the food that is needful for me, lest I be full and deny you and say, "Who is the LORD?" or lest I be poor and steal and profane the name of my God.*

Certain issues may arise where the income is scarce and help is needed. However, more money for the use of extreme personal wants can be detrimental to the well-being of a godly family. Those who trust in riches do not trust in God. Riches as our Lord sees cannot be counted in coins and paper money.

Guidelines need to be set in how much of your time devotes to the daily tasks of your business. It should not interfere with any needs of your family. Keep in mind the earnings made are to supplement the main source of income. The mother is not to become the chief provider if the father is present in the home. Hindering you in being the wife and mother God wants you to be is counter-productive. Motherhood must come first. Added stress to children makes the effort of no worth as well. If a child should develop behavior issues since the home business started, consider it may be the culprit. All new ventures require time to adjust but you will recognize if it is right for your family. Keep your priorities straight. The business should aid the family, not hamper. Do not allow the tail to wag the dog.

Questions to consider - Chapter 11

1. Who is to provide the main source of income for a family?

2. What are the advantages to having a home based business?

3. How could a home business benefit those who home educate?

4. Can you think of any other home based business which was not mentioned?

5. How will you know if a home business does not suit your family?

Chapter 12 - Living on One Income

For we brought nothing into this world, and it is certain we can carry nothing out. And having food and raiment let us be therewith content. But they that will be rich fall into tempta-tion and a snare, and into many foolish and hurtful lusts, which drown men in destruction and perdition. For the love of money is the root of all evil: which while some coveted after, they have erred from the faith, and pierced themselves through with many sorrows (KJV). I Timothy 6:7-10

Where is it written in stone all families must have two incomes to survive? How is it possible to make ends meet when one parent is the bread winner? Would that bread consist of just peanut butter and jelly? Will a family live in poverty surrounded with furnishings from the junkyard? Let us consider how to manage a one income family and live well. Not just well but vastly improve your connection as a family in closeness and come to discern the value of everything.

Here the rubber meets the road. One income families are rare. Most married women work outside the home not to pursue a dream career. Though they may enjoy their profession, the feeling of fulfillment does not spur them on. Indeed her Christian influence spreads to those whom she shares the occupation. But the truth is she works to pay bills. To help her husband pay the accounts of basic necessities becomes her work also. Did God give her that role?

To affirm our world today embraces materialism is well agreed. Having two or more of most possessions (cars, televisions, cell phones, etc.) is deemed normal and not to possess at least one seems abnormal. The greediness and gain of this culture influences our children where at young ages they assume the right for the same. Why does an eight year old child need a cell phone? Are high school students required to have their own car to graduate and receive a diploma? Must all living rooms be equipped with large, flat screen televisions connected to cable or satellite servers to keep up with news and the latest trends? As the cost of having and maintaining these items climb, we lose perspective on the bare essentials we truly need. This is why so many women feel the pull of more income. Can you live on one income? It begins with a different mindset to realize more can be accomplished with less. More of what you ask? More time together, more dependence on God, more growth in character.

Psalm 119:37-38 *Turn my eyes from looking at worthless things; and give me life in your ways. Confirm to your servant your promise, that you may be feared.*

While our children were still in grade school, we read as a family the "Little House" series by Laura Ingalls Wilder. Tears of shame came to my eyes as I learned the gift of an orange or a stick of peppermint to a child of 1870 was a great treasure. Had I not just tried to justify purchasing a thirty dollar Lego set? White table sugar was a treat not often afforded. Routinely I douse my morning coffee with a heaping spoonful. Dresses were hand-ed down mother to daughter then younger sisters until utilized as curtains.

How often had I tossed out a somewhat worn clothing item! Surely reading about life in simpler times awakens us to examine our needs and wants. Besides reading these books for literature requirements, following the Ingalls' life book by book taught us more about ourselves in the end. Even now our children recall those chapters and reflect on hardships they are blessed to not have faced. They now think twice before complaining. Find books to read on your own or with your children of early settlers or war ravaged nations. Your outlook will change.

How can we begin to save as a family and exist on one income? Make a list of things you can do without. Begin to rethink real needs contrasted with passing wants. Do this as a family so all will strive together to work towards a goal of saving and budgeting. Now you are teaching your children skills they will need and involving them in the family's well-being. When a child understands money is limited, they will be less likely to ask for unnecessary items. Start small by not purchasing the brand name shoes and then expand to services you can eliminate. Rework your budget with your husband and search hard to find the income on which you all can exist. Research how to use coupons to your advantage and save at local grocery stores. Keep an eye open for sales on needed items waiting to purchase them. Shop consignment stores for clothing items when needed. These stores will only take items in near perfect condition so the saving can be enormous compared to retail. Ask friends with children to exchange gently used clothing. Most all families are looking to save money and would happily use the opportunity to help each other.

Eat at home resisting the convenience of eating out at restaurants or fast food. That saving alone for an average size family is enough to buy groceries for days. More importantly, the quiet house as opposed to a noisy restaurant connects parents and children together at mealtime. Do you not see how this is a win for all involved? While saving money, the family is saved as well. Use the family table to talk and truly learn your children. Involve them in the preparation of the meal. Teach them to help clean the kitchen. So much good comes from this. Talking, laughing and sharing time together from meal preparation to cleaning are irreplaceable. You will not miss eating out but relish staying home.

Check out books and magazines from the local library instead of purchasing. Research online free services or products you need. Do the homework to discover how an item can be purchased at the greatest discount.

Philippians 4:11-13 *Not that I am speaking of being in need, for I have learned in whatever situation I am to be content. I know how to be brought low, and I know how to abound. In any and every circumstance, I have learned the secret of facing plenty and hunger, abundance and need. I can do all things through him who strengthens me.*

Above all, do not forget to rely on the care of God for your family's needs. Our family has lived on one income from the beginning of our marriage and as we have been blessed with three children. Situations arose where we could not fathom how we would continue to the next month. But we always did. Never have we been tossed out of a house or any gone to bed hungry. God continually cares for our family and in turn our faith grows stronger. We are sustained by God and good stewardship.

Matthew 6:31-34 *Therefore do not be anxious, saying, 'What shall we eat?' or 'What shall we drink?' or 'What shall we wear?' For the Gentiles seek after all these things, and your heavenly Father knows that you need them all. But seek first the kingdom of God and his righteousness, and all these things will be added to you. "Therefore do not be anxious about tomorrow, for tomorrow will be anxious for itself. Sufficient for the day is its own trouble.*

1 Peter 5:6-7 *Humble yourselves, therefore, under the mighty hand of God so that at the proper time he may exalt you, casting all your anxieties on him, because he cares for you.*

Let us not allow our children to drown in the flood of commercialism. There is no shame in not having frivolous items while we are blessed with the basics of clothes, food and shelter. Paul instructed Timothy in 1Timothy 6 with food and clothing we are to be content. No child will be harmed by wearing generic brands instead of the overpriced designer name for the same item. In contrast, children will flourish better not possessing certain expensive items such as smart phones, television in their bedroom and the latest game system to connect. They learn to use the mind God blessed them with and develop creativity. We all can become guilty of Paul's words in verse ten, *For the love of money is the root of all evil: which while some coveted after, they have erred from the faith, and pierced themselves through with many sorrows (KJV).* The lure of new shiny things is a great temptation. If we do not continue to check our priorities, we can easily succumb to this enticement and find ourselves in a mountain of debt.

Proverbs 23:4-5 *Labour not to be rich: cease from thine own wisdom. Wilt thou set thine eyes upon that which is not? for riches certainly make themselves wings; they fly away as an eagle toward heaven (KJV).*

Questions to consider - Chapter 12

1. Why are most families providing two incomes?

2. According to 1 Timothy 6:8 with what are we to be content?

3. Paul teaches us in Philippians 4:11-13 he learned to be content because of whom?

4. We are promised our physical needs will be met in Matthew 6:31. But what must be our priority?

5. What is compared to an eagle in Proverbs 23:5?

Chapter 13 - Reaping the Benefits of Staying Home

Sow to yourselves in righteousness, reap in mercy; break up your fallow ground: for it is time to seek the LORD, till he come and rain righteousness upon you (KJV). Hosea 10:12

Staying home becomes the most wonderful gift once a woman learns how to let go of worldly wisdom of outside career and thrive in her new horizons of domesticity. Neither a dirty word nor a mundane position, *homemaker* is defined as "devotion to home life". What better life to be devoted! Following God's commands for the home she now strengthens the family. Though schedules will still be busy and hectic, the goal and purpose has changed. No longer juggling the dual roles of mother and career woman, she can focus completely on her family and the benefit to that end.

Think of all the firsts you will see! Each small development an infant takes should be witnessed by the mother. From learning to roll over, crawl and pull up you can document every triumph in a book and by photograph. See it firsthand and reminisce as years pass. You hear the first words they begin to utter. Be the one to see the first steps of your child. You determine to teach them how to pronounce words and begin to read. Be the one to praise a piece of artwork though you are not sure which direction it hangs. All the funny phrases said and silly times together cannot be replayed the same. These little moments are what make life memorable. You will look back and not regret. You will look ahead for more joy to come.

Our first son learned to crawl reaching for the television remote. I still remember placing his toys just out of reach to generate the urge to get them in his hand. Though I tried tempting with several of his noisemakers, it was the television remote which he wanted. He eagerly reached for it and literally crawled around the room to obtain the prize. Our second son had the endearing habit of sticking his tongue out in concentration whether coloring a page or constructing blocks. His intensity in every effort has been noticeable from the start. Our daughter as a toddler routinely closed doors throughout the house in her organizational manner. I did not realize I tended to leave doors open until she taught me better. If I had not been home to witness these tiny but beautiful events, I would not have the insight into what makes up their character today. I am so thankful to have been home.

Open the door to greet them home. Hear the upsetting or thrilling day they have had. If your child is school age and attends public or private institutions, have your home ready with the warmth of welcoming arms and listening ears. I recall a sad word I learned as a girl. The term "latchkey kid" should not exist. This refers to children returning to an empty home because of parents elsewhere working. It has been documented those children can suffer loneliness, fear and behavioral issues such as alcohol and drug abuse. Sexual promiscuity becomes an issue as they grow older when they have no watchful eye. When a mother stays home, the home becomes a lighthouse in a storm. The lighthouse keeper, keeper of the home, remains steadfast and ready when needed. Keep the light on to warn of dangers outside and to shine on the good inside.

When the inevitable sickness comes to a home, a mother transforms to both doctor and nurse. A sick child needs their mother. No one cares for and makes hurts vanish better than a mother. Her gentle touch, soft voice and knowing how to comfort her child becomes the only cure when in need. Fathers reassure and steady a situation but mothers administer and heal. Mothers handily fight colds, flu and stomach virus. Knowing which medicine to dose and ointment to put on, she begins the healing process. She bandages cuts and bruises deftly. Mothers apply ice to black eyes, insect stings and sprains without a second thought. Draws oatmeal baths for chicken pox and dabs calamine lotion to poison ivy rash. Sweeping through a home she cleans and sanitizes the instant needed with her disinfecting ability. Soothing chicken soup is her main weapon. She is better than a super hero!

Proverbs 20:11 *Even a child makes himself known by his acts, by whether his conduct is pure and upright.*

Another benefit of staying home is to thwart temptation. A mother at home knows which companions are visiting and what activity happens. Danger to young children from folly is adverted. Compromising situations to older children has no opportunity. Being present at home discourages the misuse of the computer or other electronic devices. So many evils are too readily available with the click of a mouse or touch on a pad. Home computers need to be in a common area so what appears on the screen can be seen by all. Put computer safeguards on. Know what music they are listening to when headphones or ear buds are used. Make certain only approved songs enter into those ears. Temptations leave when one knows they are being watched. More importantly, they leave when given a better purpose with their time. Harness the opportunity to teach cooking skills in preparing dinner for the family. Have children help with a backyard garden. Get them involved in redecorating a room in your home.

Enjoy the time to eat together. Father can share good moments in his work or shake off stress from hearing laughter in children recounting their day. Coming together as a family to sit at the same table and partake in meals together knits members closer in love. Some of the best conversations and funniest moments occur at dinner time. I encourage you to not have the television playing at meals. That is counterproductive in communicating. Granted not every meal will be harmonious or without unkind words from siblings but as a whole the routine of family meals is productive. Preparing a meal takes thought in constructing menus, time in finding ingredients and effort in cooking the food. Your family sees the love and care you put forth. The aroma of home cooked meals remains one of the most treasured memories for many. It lets all know "my mother is home and taking care of me".

Treasure time spent together in the evening. Without outside employment, a mother continues to focus her care and time on her home. The stress of a career does not factor into her emotional or mental health. She readily plays or relaxes with her family after dinner. No work will be brought home from the office since her occupation is her home. Crouching behind the bed, I played a hide and seek game with my daughter as an infant. Quietly calling her name, she would crawl and find me, bumping her forehead to mine in a tag sort of way. She knew the sound of my voice and enjoyed playing along. To this day, she wants to hear of that memory. How many memories you can create! Sing songs together, read books aloud or play a board game. Sit outside to feel the cool evening remembering humorous days past. Know your children inside and out, not a passing or casual acquaintance, but what they esteem, wish for and wonder. You know them since you are with them.

Bedtime routine becomes a time for cuddling. Your child will not always want to cuddle so enjoy the years they allow the pleasure. Bible passages and songs, favorite books and praying as a family should be part of each night. Repeating these steps help all grow in love for each other and the Lord. Children want to pray for their stuffed animals as they learn God loves and cares for all. Our son at three years old wondered if his beloved Elmo would have a home in Heaven. What do you say? How a parent handles these situations instills a pliable heart or hard feelings later as an adult. By assuring our son God would take care of all in His will helped calm his mind. Would a mother with an outside career have the patience to think through an appropriate answer? Exhausted and stressed, she may brush off the question to get her children in bed. Homemakers are exhausted as well but do not have the outside cares on their minds to blur their focus. It is too much to ask of women. The conclusion of a family's day compares to closing a beloved book where the last page ends happily. Set this time aside to not rush so children will learn the importance of finishing days with Bible and prayer.

Though the wording may sound archaic, the truth taught in the hymn, *How Shall the Young Secure Their Hearts,* by Isaac Watts soundly states the Bible is what will guide and guard our children. The teaching is taken from several verses in Psalm 119.

How shall the young secure their hearts,
And guard their lives from sin?
Thy word the choicest rules imparts
To keep the conscience clean.
To keep the conscience clean.
'Tis like the sun, a heavenly light,
That guides us all the day;
And through the dangers of the night,
A lamp to lead our way.

A lamp to lead our way
Thy word is everlasting truth;
How pure is every page!
That holy book shall guide our youth,
And well support our age.
And well support our age.

Joshua's last words to the children of Israel encouraged steadfastness. He reminded them the benefits they enjoyed without having labored for those blessings. The same holds true for our generation! How blessed we are with a land we did not work for, towns we did not build and food we did not grow. Joshua reminds them of God's care in Joshua 24:13-15 *I gave you a land on which you had not labored and cities that you had not built, and you dwell in them. You eat the fruit of vineyards and olive orchards that you did not plant.' "Now therefore fear the LORD and serve him in sincerity and in faithfulness. Put away the gods that your fathers served beyond the River and in Egypt, and serve the LORD. And if it is evil in your eyes to serve the LORD, choose this day whom you will serve, whether the gods your fathers served in the region beyond the River, or the gods of the Amorites in whose land you dwell. But as for me and my house, we will serve the LORD.* We also need to make the choice of whom to serve and actively see our family serves the Lord. To proactively reach the goal, changes may need to be made where parents put first the saving of their family's souls. Decide today to do all you can in teaching your children the Bible, instilling godly values and principles. Should it encompass leaving a career, take the leap of faith knowing God will provide. Use the fleeting time well you are given with your children by remaining home.

Years to come your children will remember only good of childhood.

There will be no miserable accounts to tell generations which follow. Mothers who choose the option of homemaker reap a harvest of precious memories, a grateful husband, thankful children and a beautiful life. No career in the world could provide the same sense of worth. No vocation could pay her better than her child's hug. No employment equals the role she willingly completes 365 days of the year. Vacations needed but not demanded as a right. Coffee breaks welcome but often forgotten. Every holiday she works knowing no overtime pay exists. She truly loves what she does for the love of her family. She creates a home and aptly wears the name *homemaker*.

Questions to consider - Chapter 13

1. What is the definition of homemaker?

2. If we sow righteousness, we will reap mercy according to what passage?

3. Proverbs 20:11 tells us even a child knows the difference between what?

4. What memories do you have of your family being together?

5. Make a list of the benefits for the homemaker. List benefits as God sees, not the world.

www.ingramcontent.com/pod-product-compliance
Lightning Source LLC
Chambersburg PA
CBHW071828020426
42331CB00007B/1655